American's tend to sentimentalize the b[...]

— Steph[...]

Krieger has created an iridescent tomb of the body... I will be returning to these poems again and again.

— Elle Nash, author of *Animals Eat Each Other*

Surgically deep. Sonorous architecture. Dylan Krieger runs from nothing.

— Elizabeth Victoria Aldrich, author of *Ruthless Little Things*

What doesn't kill you...will eventually," says Dylan Krieger in *Soft-Focus Slaughterhouse*—a poetry collection inspired by living with chronic pain. The nightmare of being in a body is a shared nightmare only until pain becomes distinctive, eccentric. "You can't kill what I have without taking down the whole has-been animal with it." What doesn't kill you, I might add, only makes you want to die more. "We apologize for having bodies long before they bite back." Existence, at best, is palliative care. The only cure for the human condition is death. "The death drive survives...Prognosis: endless." Though pain (and suffering) may estrange us from each other, they connect us to ourselves, and in self-intimacy, even without healing, even without hope, there is grace.

— Kim Vodicka, author of *The Elvis Machine* & *Dear Ted*

Stylistically, Krieger's poetry has a rhythm like a heartbeat. Philosophically, it's an expression of the embodied consciousness. *Soft-Focus Slaughterhouse* isn't the work of an abstract mind trapped in a body; it's the conscious body on fire and hopelessly embedded in the world.

— Charlene Elsby, author of *Hexis* & *Affect*

soft-focus slaughterhouse

dylan krieger

Requests for permission should be directed to 1111@1111press.com, or mailed to 11:11
Press LLC, 4732 13th Ave S, Minneapolis, MN 55407.

Cover Art by Mike Corrao

Paperback: 9781948687263

Printed in the United States of America

FIRST AMERICAN EDITION

9 8 7 6 5 4 3 2 1

For those who take care

table of contents

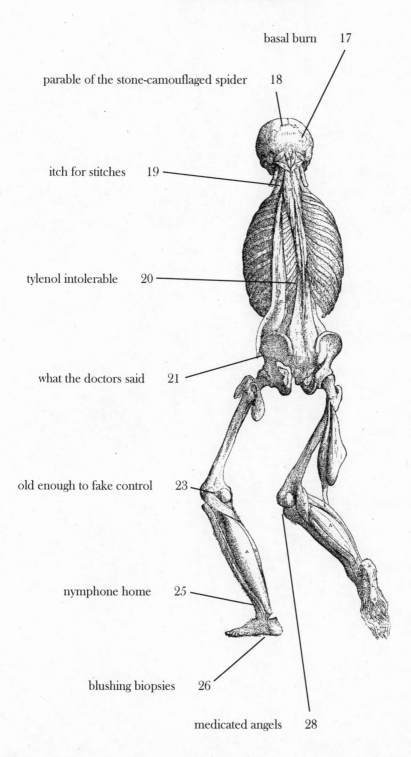

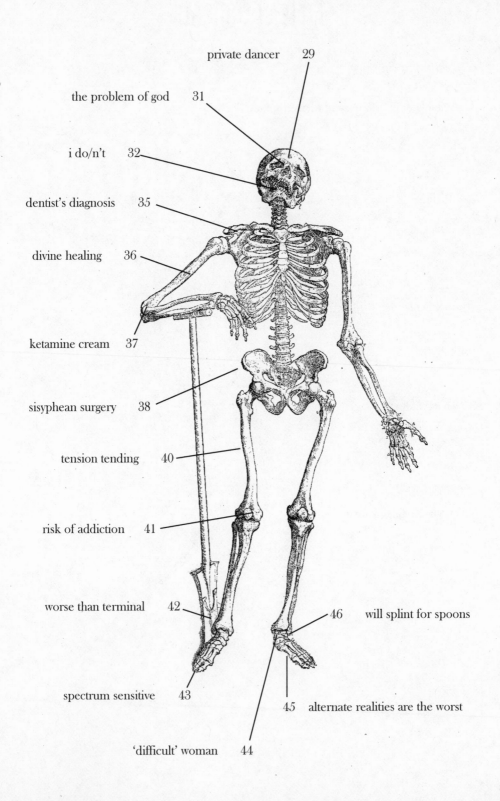

dream in which mom pulls the trigger   48

love is wanting to die together   *50*

bedside mechanic   *51*

same name, different grave   52

77th percentile   *53*

prognosis: endless   *54*

what doesn't kill you...will eventually   *56*

the trees that grew around obtrusions   58

death drive survives   *59*

misery loves doomsday   60

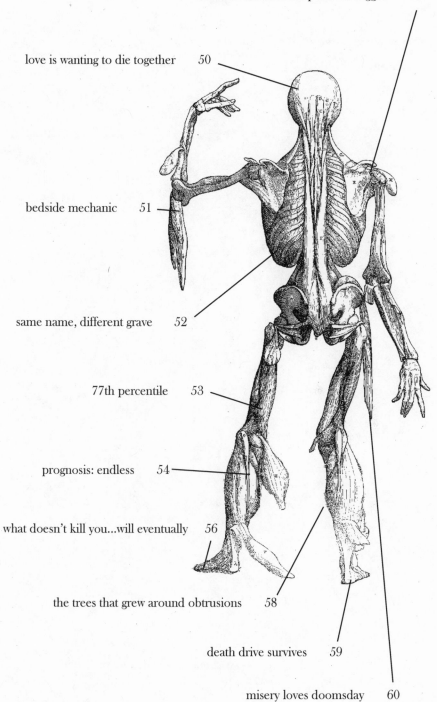

walking pharmacy/portable pothead   61

dylan downer   62

paci-fascism   64

empathy machine   65

cruelty builds character   66

the other, confronted   67

your brain on pain   69

evolution's anthem   70

eve's curse   74

all the special diets   75

meat / maker   76

drink yourself into the mood   79

biorhythms under a full moon   80

Acknowledgements

Warm thanks are due to my family for living through this reality with me, friends Alyson Phillips, Peyton (Rice) Gracia, and DeWitt Brinson for supplying or inspiring individual lines, Patrick Quigley and Vincent Cellucci for showing me what partnership amid this pain might look like, Alex Simand and Christopher Payne for reading early versions of some of these poems, Johannes Göransson and Lara Glenum for their instrumental support in my development as a writer, and all the various medical professionals without whom this book would not have been written: Drs. George Horvath, Nancy Keller-Madden, Maria Evangelista, Daniel Klauer (my diagnostic savior), and Glenn Kidder (who provided the estimate of "77th percentile"), among others.

I'd also like to thank the editors of the following journals for first publishing these particular poems:

The Collapsar ("blushing biopsies")

jubilat ("spectrum sensitive" and "all the special diets")

Nine Mile Magazine ("risk of addiction," "worse than terminal," "prognosis: endless," "the trees that grew around obtrusions," "death drive survives," "walking pharmacy/portable pothead," "paci-fascism," "empathy machine," "cruelty builds character," "the other, confronted," and "drink yourself into the mood")

West Trade Review ("private dancer" and "the problem of god")

Foreward

"a distinctly subjunctive dungeon
but here and now, in the indicative"

Let's say it's wrong to declare that(?) poetry must be about something and commend
for a moment Wallace Stevens' famous line from "The Snowman": "nothing that is
not there, and the nothing that is." We may say the poem is a neurological product.
We can say it's riven with agonies. But it's always incorrect to say a poem is fully
concerned with disablement or pain, even when it touches there. Dylan Krieger's
couplet offers the nuanced and scrupulous facts of the matter. We carry the occa-
sions of pain even as we trick them out. We cannot transcend.

Soft-Focus Slaughterhouse occupies the liminal and transgressive dungeon-indicative,
which an old Finnish shaman once described to me as "the body that isn't there that
you must conduct." Let's not read this lightly, since the poet makes no apologies for
the sharpness of the story. Americans tend to sentimentalize the body. Dylan Krieger
does not.

I've been disabled all my life. Blindness has meant daily migraine headaches and
bouts of depression. Poetry hasn't been an anodyne. One finds there are none. One
learns also that language—lyrical, subversive, wizened, spontaneous or crafted—isn't
a cure or a cop-out. Krieger writes:

> *never mind the allodynia, the burning and freezing*
> *the throb in my temple that tells me when the evening's over*
>
> *what the doctors said is they don't need me to get better*
> *just to exhaust this scripted list of possible prescriptions*
>
> *so i eat all their designer demons until my skull goes see-through*
> *until my brain leaks microwaves into the needles of forest still breathing*

It was Auden who said "poetry might be defined as the clear expression of mixed
feelings." What he didn't say is you should love your crooked body with your crooked
heart.

Take it from me: These are love poems.

Stephen Kuusisto

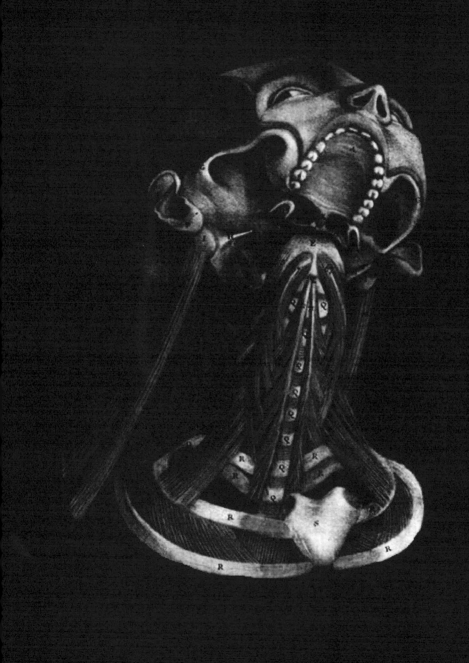

basal burn

somewhere before the teenage tipsy-after-two-drinks tingle
there was a chandelier clear within reach of my fumbling fingers

bored god of a high-flown world formed from daddy's shoulders
the icarus pissing contest begins and i decide to try my tiny hand

at winning the abyss, lick my lips like the light will be delicious
blow a kiss to all the alternate galaxies in which i didn't drink

its potion, didn't crack my skull against the concrete over and
over until it broke open, knocking loose a new ghost

from the ocean of my lonesome homeschooled cult induction
only to call it my chronic ilk, the flame that placed all its

weight on my brain until the medication was the
only way to keep the swelling vessels sane, to sing

amazing grace and mean it for another decade, until the halo
burned the faith away—he said it would all be okay, that the boo-

boo would blister, but if we whispered the right words, its wax
wings would fix with a clot and a scab—how could he under-

stand that it would never be that simple for his rumpled
little red-eyed youngest, tugging the firebrand out of the

skyline like its brightness might be worth the climb?

parable of the stone-camouflaged spider

the neighbor children had the names of hebrew priestesses: sabra and katura. in my head they were the chosen but couldn't help their house from burning. sometimes that's just how the second wife of abraham knows it's finally her turn under the billowing shroud. between the stones of our counterfeit-castle apartment complex, i stretched to squash a daddy long legs, and i don't remember which girl stopped me, but she said even the creepy crawlies counted as *god's creatures*—my first brush with shamanic shaming beyond the bounds of family bonding. but it struck me—a sharp pebble to the breastbone—every collection of cells we call alive spies its survival in the same wide-open gaseous blaze: *the force that through the green fuse drives the flower* per my namesake, moribund *hail mary*, silent plea for clever camouflage to scurry on and fuck another day, delay the grave for one more bang bang budding—no contusion, no grand piano on your throatful of champagne

itch for stitches

the centripetal pull on my pedals pulsed wrong that morning
we all heard it—the corner boy crunch of chin to gravel

have you ever seen a hound dog howl at the wrong cannibal
attack? it was like that—a riotous concussion, only quieter

a briny conspiratorial odor on every peeled-eye street sign
please excuse me for bleeding from the neck over your welcome mat

in the midwest we apologize for having bodies long before they bite back
a dozen butterfly tapings later, on the way to gymnastics i ask her

listen for the *should have* in her nonchalant hospital chatter
and under the porch swing's blown-out lantern i know we're broke but

itching for stitches, a different version of my person could have found
the fracture sooner, who could help but figure? the following

winters might have felt warmer under the mud-colored perma-cloud
where i fondled each pebble still trapped under my jawline

and made a wish on a six-candled cupcake that the ache
keeping my white space awake would efface itself from the

red-lettered spectacle of my medical record and rattle off
last rites without saying goodbye, a ripple in pink water

licking quick filth on every fishbone in my neon-wired spine

tylenol intolerable

back then i'd hover over my parents' bed
wet feathers standing on end
instead of waking them past midnight
raccoons chirping soft outside their window
where my once-watertight cranium caved
ashamed to fall prey to a pang
that couldn't dress up or red rover
itself safe—they made me swallow
eight tylenol a day for the pain
but who can make the whole wide
wilderness disintegrate into powder
into puddles? there was no affection
gathering our torsos together as we muttered
for the millennium to come for us—
only pinecones and folk songs about
how we might hammer in the mornings
a distinctly subjunctive dungeon
but here and now, in the indicative
i flick my antemeridian teardrops into
the fan-spin and breathe in sharply
through my teeth, as if the clench
of that familial muscle could lift
its skirt of perforated nerves
long enough to let me sleep

what the doctors said

what the doctors said was edible
place it under your tongue with the rise and fall of the sun

i don't recall all of it, but what the doctors said was
clearly heretical—i won't repeat what i remember, and you can't make me
(i'm acutely accustomed to torture)

what the doctors said replaced *diagnostics* with
a vacant *oh shit* and *you're not old enough to take this*

not a single one tried transplanting my amygdala with wilting lilies or
affixing charged crystals to a voodoo likeness of my visage

not the pediatrician, physical therapist, or—worst of all—the neurologist
not the CT scanner or MRI machines either, despite all their forward thinking

what the doctors said was often prompted by "headache calendars" i filled out weekly
based on my careful adolescent recordkeeping, they alternately deemed me

hysterical or the greatest living martyr of my era
but from their expressions, i couldn't tell one from the other

with a lazy glance of pity, what the doctors said was duck and cover
stay wounded, stay hungry

so you can't open your mouth or stand the lamplight any longer?
no matter, just take these liquid vitamins through a syringe

behind your blackout curtains and call me in a few thousand hours
the cowardice of my situation is this, the therapist insists:

to the extent my condition is psychosomatic
i could snap out of it at any moment with the right

healthy eating secrets and positive thinking
never mind the measurable clicking and twinging off balance

never mind the allodynia, the burning and freezing
the throb in my temple that tells me when the evening's over

what the doctors said is they don't need me to get better
just to exhaust this scripted list of possible prescriptions

so i eat all their designer demons until my skull goes see-through
until my brain leaks microwaves into the needles of forest still breathing

and there's a piece of me that loves being plugged in so snugly
to the world's outpouring pain repository

because it means i'm still possessed and seething
sharing a seed of experience with the vast kinetic underbelly of being

facing the blackness of space with my childhood nightgown billowing
in the antigravity of everybody's aching cavities forever

when i wake up from my self-induced coma, what the doctors said
way back when will have been debunked several times over

so i spread my fingers over the IVs, tubes, and telescreens
that make up my life's coda and sing their little digital melody

to vibrate my sternum at the same frequency
as your favorite moon of jupiter

remember when you told me that? i wasn't this sick yet
but i felt it coming like a molten earthquake

and stitched my eyelids to the seismic charts
that chime behind our breastplates, arc by arc

old enough to fake control

there's a time
and place
to take the plunge
into your own
full-grown
escape hatch
hand to halo
jesus saves
but from what?
when i'm
the danger
tracing sym-
metrical injuries
into my wrists
shins—the sting
is only sinful
in its sensuousness
a clean cathedral
where the sign
of the cross can
momentarily detract
from your loss
and the alabaster
blood looks so
stark against the
stained glass
scepter in the
confessional dark
every angel another razor
every priest a piece
of the peephole
who raped you
i came for the
hymns and
stayed for the
iron fist—go figure
even after leaving
i've a taste for
self-flagellating
draping the scabbing
gashes in gauze
and gawking at

that mythical
phenomenon
the body's
best at:
moving on

nymphone home

stuck that way, the pain becomes contagion, pleasure the only antidote
hello? hello? is there anyone left in the cosmos i haven't blown?

i fell in love with a drummer like that shitty wilco song and bought a corset
from a sex shop to disappear my patronymic on the shore of lake superior

an afternoon raft of loons bearing witness, i made the promise
but crossed my fingers behind my femur at the last second, skeptical stone-skipper

and rather than watch them starve, i shipwrecked the crew altogether
spelling out my pseudosexual malady on the sandbar

a self-sabotage worthy of sabbath day prostrations and satanic christenings
i savor the stain left on your mason jar from the last time

my shudder centers could be touched without setting off a neuralgia bomb
i'm not sorry for lifting anchor without warning, but still the mermaids

don't deserve your early morning shorthand, so i lurk along the outer banks
still casting nets for all the siren-mavens i could have played in different takes

blushing biopsies

when the biosphere of my body muddies
my mother waits out in the gynecologist's
lobby with a sanitary napkin and a vicodin
like, *congrats on surviving.* they slice the
skin above my clitoris and hole-punch
my cervix "to be thorough" like horses
without the breeding. see how easy
it would be to keep this secret? i don't
need your sympathy and since then
the scars have clammed up seamless
but when 20 and horny, fear death by
genital trauma, the *oh my god* of the
impossible liftoff: passion from pant-
omime, vaseline from vaginal lore
the horror is the whore you were
wouldn't recognize you curled up
in the back of your parents' crappy
sedan stretching your tear ducts
in an attempt to fit the entire fucking
fatherland—i wonder where they are
now, all the pieces of my proverbial
flower down the drain under the
operating table. paint my figure,
little freshmen, however you see fit
just don't miss the little tidbits
missing, the gapping of the flesh
over the heart's chamber of fester
over whatever tender's left

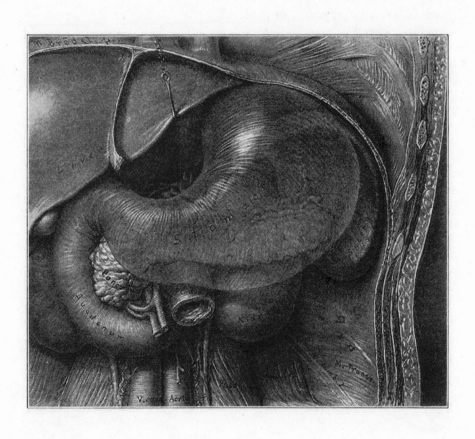

27

medicated angels

after that, my mood was made to order
zoom in on my zombie torso rearranging
all its chemicals—i dare you to follow through
on that intubation you're always ideating
i ate your prescription-strength campfire
stories and now i can't remember my own
undoing. was it the full moon with the candle-
stick in the underwater parlor? how about
we parlay the funereal drama into an anti-
dogma and empty all the coffins? i'm off
in some half-conscious fog when you ask
about the flash mob of endorphins pouring
forth from your pituitary boredom. i pump
my guts against the urge to pass out in the
alley and shiver myself to the pharmacy
what harm in it? by the time the medicine
works its magic i've had it with other kinds
of compromised lives—welcome to the
night-owl drivel stage of your demise
your addicted existence mumbling from
the bible in latin—like, who even does that?
patch me up for the crunching. no matter
what bad man wrenches my hip out of place
jacob's ladder is still just poor man's DNA

private dancer

on the steps of the chapel
ever after dismembers
all our friends and family
laugh with their backs to the
baptismal when i get dizzy
you point out where we're
sitting on the isthmus and
i kiss the tantric distance
between your hip and
happy trail failing again
at every instance
it's egregious
how i let her
my private dancer
drown out the bells
we rang together
but to be fair
she really is that loud
in the conservatory hollow
how are you now?
i'm living simply
as you predicted:
at the bottom of
a moss-tinged bottle
still hot and bothered
to the point of it being a problem
still getting into trouble
with the gods of deaths
both big and little
in this rendition i'm your killer
but there are countless others
where the reception goes public
and the only box step is ours
all dumbstruck curly q's at cute angles
no coming home from the honeymoon
to an accidental hanging
no hairpiece sewn in
to elide your own inner murderer
that glass-eyed dragon
it happened overnight
i swear you stirred
in bed and the wedding

hopped a plane to denver
hell set up shop under your
fingernails and the tall tales
won't stop spewing from my
loose-toothed grin as if
the gin is all it takes to
momentarily outpace
the makeshift ballerina
lambasting pageant crone
undead cacophony
of what's at stake

the problem of god

last chance to get nasty in the knicknack antique catholic mass
batten down your tousled curls coming out of the confessional
medieval murals move their eyes all over our speechless misdeeds
so who needs them? to call it *the problem of evil* is misleading
nothing illogical about a lion-like gnashing of fangs in a natural predator
when i said you were a monster, sure i meant it, but in a hot-to-trot way
don't get my scoff wrong: it's the concept of god that's the problem
an arbitrary authority on all things *ought* who conveniently doesn't talk?
fuck off. i plug my headphones into the west wind while all the pedants
kneeling next to me pretend to listen in for his invisible verdict on all things
mischievous or divisive—i'm divided myself when he puts a hot
poker to my insides the same year my only extended family dies
it's enough to knock the cross out of my coddled college nightlife
and codify the plight of *soulmates* as just another faceless virus

i do/n't

wish you'd really been the morning

press my flesh against every ashtray

hoping we'll become family

keep kosher on your birthday

just to set it aside in some way

patiently unchange my name

under the hourglass of your remains

aim a shotgun at the sun

every time a dark puddle

bungles a streetlamp reflection

have sex with more sinkholes

than this sentence can hold

boldly venture to the border

of this abominable tectonic altar

to barter with our tentacled forefathers

clotting thickly at the sting sores

but the survival imperative means more

than just tallying miraculous births

what passes for pansies lining the aisles

is only painted satin and plastic

a taxidermist's trickster stab at happy

and we the stranded gentry

clipped and glamoured

hands hooped huge

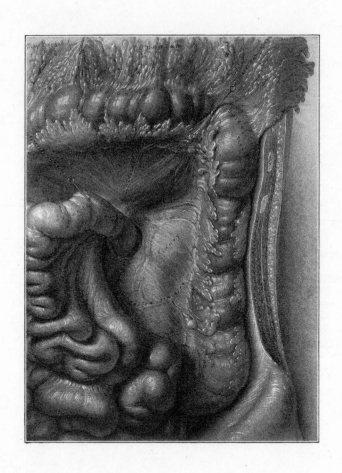

dentist's diagnosis

in all the scans, my masticators begin to eviscerate themselves
bruxism upon bruxism until i'm labeled parafunctional

i stand with my shoulders back against the hallway wall
in need of a patchwork root canal and they jot down

every minor resulting deformity, more necessary recordkeeping
and it hurts to hear the hygienists sing their little tune about you

like you're not in the room, but it gets catchy eventually
against your better judgment, when the outro is an answer

that long-awaited foghorn blasting: *anterior jaw dislocation
with reduction*—how lovely, the un-music of it, the listless way

science can pinpoint fate without a single rabbit skinned
in the plot for my escape—the splint they sell me for $2,000

is only a preventive measure for cracked molars
no reform for the porcelain joint that unhinged

its wisdom for the taste of a highrise, mirroring the city's
crooked spires with an eye toward leaving them behind

divine healing

over and over and over: *like Job*
to suffer unjustly is to see the face of god

a bursting at the carcass
a blurring barcode

what we cannot purchase
i stick my fingers in the temple

of my body and pray the way
the tax collectors taught me

collapsing ecstatically
against the sound of trapped

music and a gravestone
ever so slowly

starting to mean nothing
i feel the preliminary tremor

cranial freewheel
porous curlings of grey matter

returned to burning equilibrium
and by the time i board the train

my baseline standards for who i let
get me naked changes

and i'm not even kidding
. when i say all i'm wearing

under my charred skirt
is the tangible proof i'm not faking

i carry the x-rays around like a namesake
and make believe i'll breach this wave of

psalms with all my skin still on

ketamine cream

there's a store around the corner where they make the feel-good scraps from scratch

apply liberally to affected area as often as needed or until the skin's rubbed raw

leave all your old friends in the comments section of your death

there is no fingering the sticky cartilage in hopes the injury unlearns its curdle

i make a fist tight enough to hurt myself for every drug i thought might help but didn't

and dare to stay awake for the warcry of whatever scalpel comes after

sisyphean surgery

even as beleaguered seekers speeding down the runway of scientific research
we can't touch this. you reach into your back pocket and block a bullet with
your pinky finger, but no, you still don't know how to reattach a free-floating
arthritic disc to the bony hinge above my throat—at least not without its click
bait of a widget slipping out again—so i figure i'll try every other hot
cure in the bloat show, siphon seraphim out of a syringe, and lo and behold:
no dice. i'm in the outhouse after midnight when i spot a black bear through
a crack in the door and wonder whether it would be better not to be tempted
by the specter of medical intervention, to be feral, hair raising straight from the
spinal cord like a stegosaur. i hear myself on the megaphone, a traffic cone
toppled over by the side of the road, but the passing cars and herd of stags
skirting a nearby forest don't even take notice. the construction workers won't
bother to right me either, i promise. just like the doctors, they know despite all
semblance of progress, some feeble cannibals aren't worth their weight in sausage

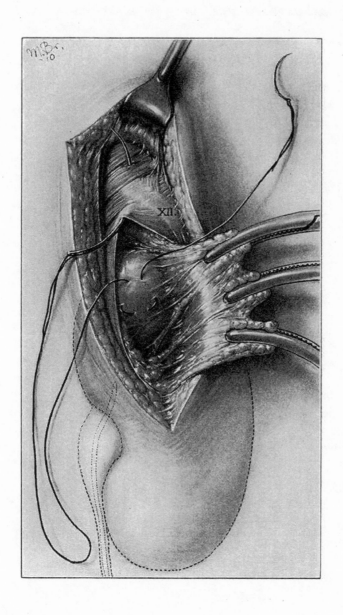

tension tending

despite my best attempts, the clenching only intensifies

and what's the surprise? trying, after all, is a stretch

squint to see better, bend your neck toward teacher

hoist your hand to reach the low-hanging answers that have us cornered

in the old world, there would have been a word for when

the cortisol and adrenaline ramp up in the hunt, but nowadays

it's par for the cubicle—blood on blood, i pick the scabs clean off

because it's what my mother would have done, a perfectionist's self-

defeating incision, chipping more and more marble floorward

to make it even until there's nothing left to call a sculpture

of course i heard you when you said the muscle relaxant/xanax combo

was a bad idea, but i did it anyway and then told you a story about

a ghost town surrounded by enchanted skulls and antlers

forcefield penetrable only by the archangel of morphine

risk of addiction

sick, yes, but not to death
that would be too easy
a remedy in and of itself
they stick a secret needle
in my IV and for a second
i forget i'm screaming
the cheap hospital sheets
play on my pain receptors
but by then i'm elsewhere
too numb to care
if we're being honest
i could get used to this
the silent drama of the nausea
storming my internal sewers
the chewed-up whiplash of a
sleepy slapdash chemical solution
what a rush, to trust
the intravenous genius
of the poppyseed
to bind my fluids
truncate the once-useful
bruising of the brain
for a future stage of evolution
and here i am, young hopeful surgeon
able to converse calmly without
howling out our mutual ruin
at least until the comedown
soberly feared, highly fabled
slo-mo draconian car chase
no lucky junkie can outpace

worse than terminal

i first heard this sentiment on a right to death website

every sympathy has a shelf life

gather round the water cooler if my disease approaches climax

fast enough to follow with your finger through the fiscal quarter

but after five years eavesdropping on the word *chronic*

there's no hiding you're bored

no number of shoulder massages or polite *i'm sorry*'s will exactly "work"

if by that you mean a coverup of what will never come

you can't kill what i have

without taking down the whole has-been animal with it

i'm woke enough to know i will miss being owned

and when they put me to sleep they'll peer in through the loose seams

and see the freakout of my connective tissues

itching to lock onto some eccentric medic's leash

spectrum sensitive

you pick up a wanton signal in your nerve endings and morse code a cagey greeting. no telling who is calling. jekyll or hyde, a fuckboy gemini who keeps you crawling across his awful x axis for the mythologized prospect of y. i once made my mother cry by telling her my personal record—how many times i came at the hand of a man in a day. so maybe the pain is just the inverse of a broader spectrum of sensation—spread my legs and you can see the range. for every sunroof rager, a backseat hangover. for every butterfly, a battered wife. the danger of counting your blessings is drinking buddies will never outnumber the date-raping strangers you can stomach. you keep waiting for the moment you get full enough to vomit, but after a decade in the touch-me trenches, you suspect it's never coming. cut me open across the abdomen and watch them all fall out on the linoleum, untold reverse births half-digested at the fontanel. if my body is a temple, fix a bell to your sandal. jingle like hell

'difficult' woman

all the lab coats promise there's a logic to this diagnosis, even if no one can find it. comb me over and slather on the pesticide until my thorax divorces my antennae. why does every routine checkup devolve into a CAT scan contest? some people think i've gone septic on purpose, but that omits half the story. a stolen purse dumped on the subway, my rotting contents are the best clue to whose foul play gaped me ugly. if i report my badmouth ransacked, would you call me dramatic, a high-maintenance patient? sometimes even when you're silent, your stethoscope pokes out to say something. the exoskeleton of stoicism, a frozen metal with a hard-on for its own reflection. help me upturn my hundred tongues to hum the problem as loud as possible to the heavens. and if it's too much to watch me keep digging through trash for what stings, just turn around your gaslights and pretend it isn't happening

alternate realities are the worst

we imagine the universe as organized by osmosis

watch me bleed into the seaweed and vice versa

soon as you drop your keys down a sewer grate

it's already too late to press your semipermeable

membrane against the nauseous ambivalence of fate

you are mourning that alternate reality in which

you see your killer coming all along, screen for cancer after

every casual power plant meltdown, grip the steel

ring with your name on it tight enough to fight the slip

what is the so-called human condition if not this

bittersweet ability to fill in the nonexistent with cinematic color schemes

and agonize at the tension between the tree's branches

as if only one thin limb away from world peace or

that sexy edenic secrecy between undressed bodies

becoming one with the leaves—this is the fantasy

your parents warned you about, where the milk

was never spilled, wrong answer never uttered

teeth never shattered by concrete, inches from safety

that paradise cannot be retraced, the grownups tell us

so don't pummel your pretty little head against the unnecessary dead

what could or could not be evaded from space

even a thread of the fabric remains too large for your jaws to contain

will splint for spoons

if you haven't noticed

i have an unabashed idiolect

and i'm not afraid to use it

before the cops escort me home

real slow in the name of the lord

i spell yours out in silver at the diner

but you just bus the table like normal

i'd hold you like a secret locket but

the splint is for keeping everything separate

gum tissue from gladiating masticator

dental dam from kingdom come

when you called it *all in good fun*

you were crossing two spoons

behind your back the whole time

did you think i wouldn't notice

your distraction tactics like an orthodontist

vibrating the side of my face for the injection

order me off-menu, maintain eye contact

while i drive up the value of this garbage upholstery

it's irresistable to start eating myself

if not for the metal contraption in my mouth

you are all that's left and what's saddest

is the taste of our bloodlust blending

and all the presidents i'd kill for it

dream in which mom pulls the trigger

it dawns

                    on no one in particular

this town is too ghost

                        to decompose

there's a convenience store

                          where we ignore

who's who in all this

                        hellbent holy

you hold a gangbanger's

                          daughter hostage

until he quids your quo

                        presses a metal barrel

against my gospel

                  of bad posture

scofflaw scandal

                      waiting to happen

and just to pander

to the passing banter

of pimped children

you snuff me yourself

expert headshot to the temple

in this rendition of heaven

do not collect $200

do not call a boardwalk home

love is wanting to die together

eyelash to eyelash, unembarrassed by the reverberation of inside splashing outside
i doubt this is what the cakemaker imagines when selecting miniature bridegrooms
but it's true: the family member i oh-so-ceremoniously choose myself
will be the shamanic monster who can read the patterns in my ashes
and tell you which unconscious condiment my disembodiment is hungry for
how many licks it takes to make my windows shutter
even godless, i still wonder whether such a hard boundary
between seduced animals can survive in perpetuity
not just for anyone, but for my specific collection of meat and steam
a secret sapling going to seed all over both our tundras until your deathbed
is just the other endzone of my selfsame invisible vineyard
last breath a careful how-to on the frequency
of waterings, the depth of permafreeze

bedside mechanic

step-by-step instructions for dummies:
how to fix your chronically sick significant other

mash your sense organs into their lap—act sad
puff out your chest to demonstrate you are

the single most melancholy mammal in indiana,
atlanta, what have you. watch the petty waft

of competition soothe their aching muscles
pass a bus station and sigh like you will never

see the world's wonders. learn how to make
their favorite meals paleo, vegan, soy-free

the doctors will demand it sooner or later
but be patient—you have your whole lives

to hate this game, not the player. savor the
mundane safety of movie night, sexy time

special occasions unsullied by hyperventilation
through clenched teeth, the numbing powers

of alcohol and marijuana, the all-too-often
impossible foreplay in public, distraction by

train track, childlike mischief on rooftops—
stop me if this is too much. i just want

someone to care enough to drop me
off a cliff and and let the stormy weather

parachute my dress into a poultice for
my nervous system's pulsating unrest

is that too much to ask? after the rains
pass, i promise we'll kiss as if it's painless

and i'll whisper to the western wind who mended me
with only a socket wrench and a high-flying trapeze

same name, different grave

inspired pyro, you must have fabricated a thousand forest fires
for the forcefield of trashy block parties we call a city

hit me in the face and say no other dumb mutt yelps the same
the solipsism of others makes us linger in dingy alleys

waiting for the fickle felon with enough blood under his fingernails
to make my first kiss ring of criminality on a discarded sofa

separated years ago from its loveseat, this ghetto beckons, baby
hear me when i tell you i'm getting thin enough to lose everything

i gained from puberty and go back to that dumpster of stuffed animal laughter
sure, i'd miss the liquor and the expert perversion of clicking my tongue

against your every body part, but we could still share a mouthful
of hot chocolate in december, when the lake effect snow gets too tall to handle

and our bottomless want floats up the chimney with its smoky tendrils
only one ending of several, rest assured, little devil

77th percentile

some like to watch
i prefer calculating
the likelihood of the landing

the bird spread
hawked down and
waiting on the wing

the spitball must be
perfectly arced
curve in all the right spots

to land atop the spiked
punch bowl at the black-eye
event of the semester

ok, you caught me
only messing
i never went

not to the events, tests
or even a proper high school campus
my sister and i were busy

pulling the bible from our ears
and dropping it down sewer grates
but i kept a little for my headaches

no one could blame me
and it helped one day out of 10,000
which puts me in the 77th percentile

of patients with recurrent inflammation
and the will to keep count
over and over again

a roadside wreck as the crow flies
then another
then another

there is nothing more
to see here
move along

prognosis: endless

viruses and diamonds:

    getting better

home among hot coals

    growing old

yet refusing to molt

    revolt

take your rape out

    disintegrate

in this apocalypse

    i'm basically

and the singing really

    outside a

permanently pegged

    but unlike

the song stopped

    watching

the perennials end

    begin

a tale of never

    making a high-pressure

in your spinal cord

    surrounded by all your fine feathers

strip to your skivvies

    skin sack to skin sack

in the rain and let it

    there's a saying for how to stay sane

but i've forgotten it

    a potted plant at this point

does work wonders

    pharmacy in florabama i had you

an unremittent coastal quake

    the fibromyalgia, allodynia

edge of my seat

    the hoarfrost for where

and my seasonal demons

    turning tail

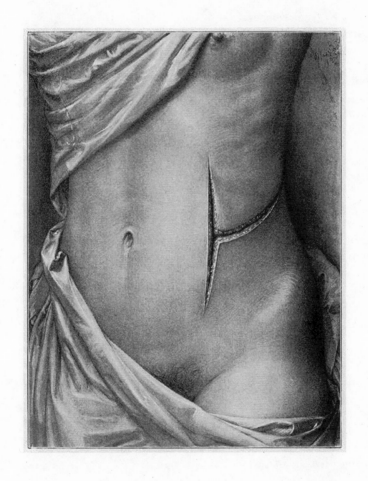

what doesn't kill you...will eventually

there is a prescience in the pitter-
patter of my pain receptors

some tissues connective even
beyond the confines of the body

find me a dick as many inches as
the average snowfall in this city

find me a dumpster fire that
isn't candid-cammed by satellite

when you're this sick this early
the predictions don't look good

the cartoonists start to sketch you with
dark shadows caterwauling about your head

and you learn all the world's different
doctrines of death: god the father

allah, buddha, brahma, heraclitus
but the future has always been nihilist

hospital chic, meaningless miles of
forest peppered by parking lots

i've never had the pleasure of
coming from or into money but

i'm educated enough to know nothing
begets nothing—and no, cordelia

isn't breathing, the universe doesn't
love you, the pizza grease isn't

trying to tell you something
sentience is an accident

and i can't decide whether we hit
the jackpot or some more sinister

lottery à la shirley jackson
but no matter the outcome

after the cat scans catch up to you
you'll still wake up every intervening

morning waiting on some godot
cracking jokes about hangmen

as it's the only stone to throw

the trees that grew around obtrusions

rapidly approaching
the warpspeed/burnout
coin toss   i offer up
our crooked childhoods
those sad saplings
stretching their tendrils
around their own undoing
immovable bench or
boulder trying its damnedest
to stunt the up-and-coming
the mother of invention
is a bitch   but what of it?
in her vitriol is a continuity
with that rusty blood color
of the earth in the south
you've got to respect that
about clueless tourists
at least they know
when to step back
and let the world
eat out its murders

death drive survives

the daymare disrobes
as follows:

cozy up
to a headstone

this could take all year
in the churchyard where

no two bones are brothers
something about *coming clean*

always sounded dirty to me
the paradox of fucking

off and on in one slow motion
the domes of great prophets go

crunch in a box just like the rest of us
sell my pen name to the end-times

who else craves the last gasp
of this planet as we know it?

the blackout is beautiful
i assure you

everyone is doing it
you don't even have to

know your blood type
or resting heart rate

to vacate the seen-straight
with your larynx hanging out

and play the ancient no-more-pain game
for a soft-focus slaughterhouse

misery loves doomsday

my main priority these days is not to drink myself into extinction
too easy to disagree on the tone of silence over telephone wires
you say there is a group that meets on tuesday nights out past
the microbrewery and the pirate-themed dive, but you see the problem
before i have to say it—this is still the public intox state and my
homeschooling has doomed me to feel like the poet laureate
of inappropriate stories in every stranger-filled room i set foot in
so instead i make friends with the reflective shapes behind the bar
carve out a little pod for myself and my drooping petals against the far wall
and ask you whether there's a program for people obsessed with armageddon
like are we just supposed to shoulder this burden all on our own?
the purified water and firewood can get heavy, and it's hard
to tell the difference between real and fraudulent extraterrestrial invasions
let's get together in person, like a cultish commune but cooler
and swap a few bottles over what may or may not occur
after the revolution rolls in and before it washes us ashore

walking pharmacy/portable pothead

the haze behind my eyes was draped there for a reason
open up my mary poppins hospital bag and behold valhalla
uppers   downers   dusters   dancers   seers   shooters
assume anything edible harbors effects on your head space
anxious? nauseous? how about just plain obnoxiously sober?
don't you fret, the devil's here now, manifesting as manic pixie
turned abject mess of a human being—*don't call her an addict
or she'll get all uppity about chronic pain conditions*—i imagine
people whisper these things, but really i'm not that important
at the corner drugstore, however, i'm the ominous transfiguration
of adulthood into paranormal tantrum, dark makeup laughing
over loudspeaker: the secret to not killing yourself is oxy
moronically, dying countless times a day until your lips
unlock lost wisdom, until staying in business becomes
an exercise best left to potted plants and other non
nomadic   freaks of fortune

dylan downer

i stick my heart out on a power line
only to realize it will freeze there overnight

bottom doesn't feel so low unless
fallen from an optimistic height

shellac the abandoned dock of my body
what's lost? is a question everyone

keeps under glass like a ship in a bottle
i box-step by myself

into the forest, floored to death
bad influence isn't the accusation

i expected, but now i'm proud of it:
rebel student in youth group, curled up

fetal position, lips painted & pierced
fear the shepherd who filibusters for

attention at the pulpit i scatter my shorn hair
fornications in the pastor's office

a born con artist without a conscience
in comparison to the floggings i've witnessed

your *negative* label doesn't mean much
but for once i'll admit you were right

i am the very hellfire i don't believe in
patting myself on the back for my treasons

if i cease to exist—passed out facedown
without you in a walmart parking lot

the starlight will still refract unabashedly like
we were mad to ever doubt it

the christmas pageants will still pretend
there's a difference between black & white

magic and the magi will still stand there
idly eyeing the manger like maybe

the audience won't notice some
frankincense left in pocket

paci-fascism

while mom & dad   slow clap   fox news

the slinky from last christmas   finally makes it to the basement

and my sister & i   strike matches   in what we once called

the coal room but nothing   combusts like it's supposed to

the word *divorce*   twinkles but   fizzles out on our lips

and we begin naming all   the elephants piling up

behind the fridge   i'm against   violence but the urge

to eye-for-an-eye grownups   who abuse power is a bitch

86 the taste   of concussion   i'm glad i no longer

remember what we were   told we'd wronged or broken

something about   crying over   a non-physical malady

well here it is, mommy   dislocation between

the ophthalmic &   mandible   bet it matches

the curve of your palm   under a microscope

step right up to   the bone show   be my guest

it isn't pretty, how i live   attracts   ants

under the spotlight   to be extinguished   with their twitchy little limbs

empathy machine

when i visit the midwest
eerie overcast and fragile branches
farmhouses fading past horizon

you are both earnest parent and wily child
whitman was right about the multitudes
they always misinterpret dirty talk

as an invitation to reverse the seven of pentacles
but all the fruits of my labor
couldn't change you

into a parade float, so i hang back
with my long face and the quiet
knowledge we must contain

several of the same people, one bastard or another
hanging from the rafters, i'm going to whisper
a dizzy melody into your ear now

are you ready?
no one
ever is, really

if you're looking for honesty, check another tavern
this is sorcery, the story not so much
true as an illusory boondock

somewhere too untouched to tell the difference
between our separate pain centers
flashing incendiary colors

the ripples in our puddles mirror each other
and when you're swapping out
my bandage for the winter

i'm almost glad to rot

cruelty builds character

this is the saddest maxim i can manage
what's the exact right amount of deer in the headlights?
of interlocutor pressure on the knot but not the muscle?

mother never taught me what the doctors wanted
to disclose: the family history of my hip bones
the late-onset schizophrenic hormones

the scotch-drinking comes with irish silence included
i'm not sure if i've ever met anyone i would call
well adjusted, but if such a thing exists it comes

with fewer addictions and flying fists—the hardship
is what holds us hostage in or out of the hospital
hopscotching in circles forever—behind the times

perhaps, but ahead of the apocalypse—too cagey
to get close to anyone but a chainsaw and a crystal ball
all i'm saying is i know it's problematic

but i find damage attractive, so yes it sucks to suffer
but would the soft fur of suburbia be preferable?
i'm not actually as sure as you might figure

even after the hairpin whiplash of college parties
and their guarded powders, miracle of miracles
my mouth can still open all the way like a

mint-condition human, the nurses tell me
i was lucky and i place your fingers just below
my cheekbones and let you catch the swing

unhinge in one direction, and the sex is better
after that—no contest—i've shown off my weak spot
rolled over in the sandbox, i am brimming with

the juices of surrender—here, feel, touch

the other, confronted

let the layers have a life of their own

i ran out of drugs so i cat-called the fog:

the hottest part is
you could kill me
and i wouldn't stop you

as long as the episode ends with

no one getting arrested or

dolled up for work the next morning

still tripping in the periphery hoping

no one will notice how recently

we rinsed off the whiskey

zen arsonists in furs swapping

bottomless throat tricks

hint: quit all the useless struggling

and get hungry for motion sickness

when i told you i was   *all in*

i meant you are the biggest thing

i could spend the rest of my nights

attempting to   swallow entirely

sputtering with full lungs like

this way? maybe? but never enough

to catch the car our pack of dogs

tails trembling for centuries:

fenderless human skull hollowed out

for this particular predicament:

articulating   why i'm wet

your brain on pain

this is for the blood stain on the mercedes in the alley

only you can name your rapist   after contraband

do a handstand for the depth of upset that keeps

even deathbeds   absent of confession

sometimes it's better to just stare out the window

dissociate the date away like no weapon could ever

impale you, like there's no such thing as genuine

affection so this imitation must be good as any

under your head wound, there's a famished menagerie

of electrical circuits left on just to be screwed with

i wish i were kidding—imagine if there were a way to

fumigate without suffocating all the burn victims

along with the vermin—i hate being a *her* sometimes

little boxes i don't fit in   ticky tacky on the hillside

but without their common blueprint, how would i intuit

where to let my leaking brainpan   off its leash

when you're on top of me, heavy and heaving

in the hallway   of haute ruins?

evolution's anthem

tell it like it isn't
the precise
danger of
embodiment:
without pain
no foolproof way
to preserve the
body's soggy
pillow on a
mildewed platter
no discernible
signal from
nerve to spinal
column it begins
with an ending
a tributary
branching out
the river of
my cerebellum
says nothing
but protects
its vegetable
fiber flawlessly
bawling in the
basement i take
a breath and
try to remember
what evolution
meant by
establishing this
correspondence
between vicious
and viscous
that *kiss kiss*
hit me like you
mean it sensitivity
but i'm a skinny
white girl under 30
so when i slither
my hands down
my pants it's not
pathetic but sexy

and you catch me
self-objectifying
under the egg-
carton ceiling
bathroom sink
dripping out its
listless indifference
smearing my lipstick
with spittle i'm sick
and this time
you're not even
sure if i mean
physically or
just perverted
the kind of person
who perches atop
a rockface for the
sake of predation
i don't take the rain
seriously except
on days when
my own pulse
shakes my face
into a sob and
all the animals
whose throbs
once jostled them
loose from a lion's
jaws loiter just off
screen as if to tell
me all my demons
are just showy
chemistry a pendulum
of readymade injuries
drawing invisible
grimaces behind
plastic who cares
what the truth is?
the only wing
without misprints is
the trauma ward
gorgeously rendered
in ultra HD and who
would choose to

roost here given
any elevator
past the avalanche
given a mineshaft
lined with rhinestones
reflecting nothing
but itself

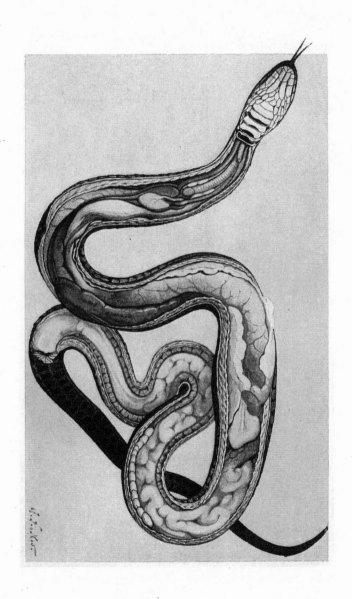

eve's curse

last-minute god in the machine

when you hit me in the temple

anvil-heavy i go rabid with headlong romantic abandon

after the gyroscopic revel, there is only a bathroom floor

where nothing matters and the thunder clapping

its happy ass like there is no new orleans left to miss

maybe our downfall was never an accident but sly sabotage

yes sometimes i'm an atomic bomb but goddammit

if i can't make a garden out of the blast

yes i'm an agony engine but i promise

to drive the whole species down with me

burrowing this barren farmland where

only the devil gets to dream

all the special diets

a mammal that can't drink milk
fetishizes its own kidnapping
like wouldn't a mysterious
disappearance be just delicious?
amber alert for my inner pseudo
patriotic glutton, it's thanksgiving
and i don't even give a shit about
pigskins or the immaculate scalpings
from which we descend—the last time
i ate turkey i was 14 with big plans for
carving up my pale wrists in the dark
there wasn't an animal in my stomach
but you for 8 years after that—naturally
i get attached, but the doctor says next
to cut out all sugars and yeast, so i bake
you into a fruit pie i can never eat and
watch you grow miniature colonies of
rot around your latticed crust going
to tragic waste untasted and i'm sure
you hate me but please keep listening
for the dinner bell because you're all
it ever talks about i swear it edges on
obnoxious honestly, sitting here starving
mouth awater at a nationstate of larva

meat / maker

from mushroom to mushroom

hallucinating nuclear warfare

one hit wondering

what else we can hellscape

in this universal murder

i'm unlearning every lens cap

stop the gyroscopic sky

from skinning itself

daily workout regimen

of drugs and alcohol

there are several people in my head

i refuse to sleep with

but they never take no for an answer

meanwhile i forge an alliance

with the drywall

swallow all the silly reasons

i still log onto your netflix and giggle

at your "continue watching"

like i could see myself

sucking your dick to that in another life

too bad the forest always grows over

where two people once knew each other

down on all fours on the dance floor

tonight i'm the kind of girl

they hold in place and bar the door for

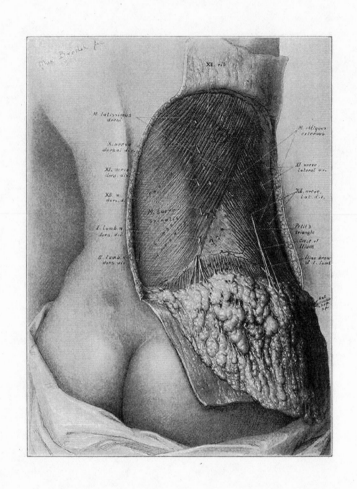

drink yourself into the mood

some days louisiana is my soulmate
just by selling me the right cognac
and smiling at my shaky face melt
no judgment from the river or
curbside buskers in the quarter
every morning a hungover heron
fishes toxic prey from the lake
like it's mocking me for drowning
my neuralgia in a watered-down
to-go cup my libido needs to function
no offense to anyone's seduction game
my body is only able to accommodate
one headstrong throb at a time
the suicidal or the sexy kind
pleasure-survival or the death drive
but somehow when you choke me
tight enough my fright combines them
full-on phobia fetishists and we laugh
late into the night at the flimsiness
of intracellular life, admire our
respective viruses for shouldering
the next extinction-triggered takeover
maybe they never saw us coming
but we did, over and over the arm
of the sofa a poorly upholstered
token of affection for happy hour
drink specials and the bareback
danger of your roommate getting
home any minute i'll miss that
black bayou inside you but by
dawn the awful birds returning
will remind my jaw to jumpstart
its hurting and everything will
trickle back to normal between
the gulf and my outpouring of
murky mass-produced daiquiris
between the secrecy of my
disease and·everyone i wish
would touch me at the shoreline
deep in the duckweed
where i can't scream

biorhythms under a full moon

the tidal twinge

comes to no conclusion

but exploding

sure it's the stuff of myth

the stiff high-up still-

reached-for light source

but there is nothing realer

under a starless stickup

we're in the thick of the abyss

the earth bears witness

to my woozy inner ear

vertigo exploding into the

lonely flush of oceans

don't go yet, reader

stay a little longer

hook yourself up

to the medicinal drip

press your lips against

my aching ribs

breathe in deep

eat all the coded signals